DNA—THE HEALING THERAPY

DNA—THE HEALING THERAPY

Create Your Life New Every Day by Choice

Kathy P. Reddick, Psy.D.

Kravitz and Sons LLC
204 E Arlington Blvd. Suite B
Greenville, NC 27858

Published by Kravitz and Sons LLC.

ISBN: 979-8-89639-667-3 (sc)
ISBN: 979-8-89639-666-6 (e)

Library of Congress Control Number: 2026910113

The opinions and instructions expressed herein are solely those of the author. Each individual should seek the advice of his or her own physician before starting any new medical program.

Table of Contents

Preface

Caution! This process will change your life.

You are about to travel into a life-changing process. If you follow the four-hour shifts as outlined in this book, your personality will shift in ninety days.

Do you wake up in the morning wondering why others are more successful than you are? What is your first thought when you wake up each day? Has it been the same for the past fifteen, twenty or thirty years? Do you seize each day and every moment when you are with people? Do you feel sad or glad, or do you even feel anything when you are with people? Would you like this to change?

If you are wondering how all this is possible, all you need to do is look to the building blocks of what makes you uniquely you. When you are born, your cells begin a journey to take care of you the way your DNA dictates, according to science. However, these little cells have a mind of their own and they can shift. If you facilitate help every four hours, you will begin to have new experiences and notice a huge difference in yourself. You will learn easier, speak differently and blow others away by the way you look every day.

The key to success is consistency. You must be rigorous in the four-hour therapy outlined in this book, especially when working with children. Every one of us has great intelligence. However, we need to discover that wisdom, that innate intelligence. To uncover the sleeping giant within is ever so important. This book will open your channels to discovery.

For the past twenty years, I have been on a mission of self-discovery. Everything I have done has led me down the path that I am now introducing to you. It hasn't always been easy. After my divorce, I began working different jobs. When I was thirty-two, while still working, I also started my bachelor's degree. I completed it ten years later. Five years after that, I completed my MBA, my DCH, and my Psy.D degree (in 2005).

What I found during those years was that no matter what was going on—a bad business deal, a lousy relationship, whatever life had in store for me—I would press on. No matter what, I would persevere. How was it possible?

At that time, I was using a combination of hypnosis, transcendental meditation tapes, essential oils and Dr. Back's remedies. I began to offer these same modalities to my clients and their problem teenagers. And damned if they did not have some major breakthroughs no matter what their upbringing, no matter how angry they were or how bad their situation! As I continued to observe these breakthroughs, I noticed that while each of the modalities alone worked well, my clients often needed an extra boost to keep going. That is when I realized that if all four modalities were an important aspect of the overall process. As Dr. Bach notes, if you treat the personality, the person will get well.

The process outlined in this book is life changing. So, be ready for more success! Be ready to be motivated and to have more fun in your life. We all want to get the very best out of ourselves, but how do we do it? This book will help you produce results that no one will believe. The results come from you. It is always you doing the process. Breakthrough will be a daily part of this process. Your productivity in all areas will rise. From now on, you will win at life!

DNA—THE HEALING THERAPY

Introduction

Awakening

We need to take back our power—the power we are to do all things in life. We must persist in our ability to have goals, desires and an all-out passion for living. We have all but lost our zest for living. How and why we lost this, I'll never know, but I have spent many years of my life discovering myself over and over again, only to find out I had the right stuff all along. I would take a seminar and at the end of all the training and motivation, I would hear a message to myself, a small voice whispering in my ear: *You had it all along.*

Each of us is our name, and with our name lies the passion that we are. We need only to tap this passion daily to recover it. We are all Einsteins and Bill Gates at heart. To realize this, it's only a matter of waking up our mind, body and soul. We may need some extra help. Being consistent is the golden key to a better way of thinking and being. We can all awaken our sleeping giant within to create a better life for ourselves.

Inner Knowing

We are on the verge of shifting our societal thinking in regards to what we do when we have a problem. When faced with a problem, you may begin to ask yourself: Is there a way I can help myself naturally? Do I personally have the ability to help heal myself mentally and physically?

The truth is that we all know ourselves. People can heal all problems. But where do we start?

I always recommend starting with a personal evaluation. Begin by taking an inventory of your life and identify the areas in which you need help. Be sure to include personal, business and social realms. Ask yourself some of the following questions: What area is out of balance in my life? Do I need more relaxation? Do I need more fun or more vacations? Do I need more quiet time? What about my family? What should I do to have more time with my family? Will I be more productive if I do all these things? Most importantly, what about my health? How can I consistently be healthy on a day-to-day basis?

For professionals reading this book, it is vital to know that your conversation with your clients is of utmost importance. When speaking to clients, you will find that they will divulge the full nature of the problem—of either their own life or their child's life.

It's always up to the client to do follow up or follow through. People become better because they have the consistent desire to do so. They listen with eagerness to your information by where your heart is. They feel your desire to help them to be better.

People are looking for a more valuable way to handle life. Most often, they need extra help to feel better physically and mentally. They only resist things that keep persisting in their lives. Sometimes they feel isolation from the problem is the key, but that's not the key. Facing the problem head on is the key. The ultimate key is forgiveness right in the moment the transgression happens. If we forgave each other moment to moment, we would not need antidepressants.

My Story

To begin, let me share a bit about my background. I have a master's degree in business and a doctorate in clinical hypnosis. I have been practicing hypnosis for fifteen years. With my work, I believe I am a pioneer in the field of energy medicine, on the forefront of what science will some day discover—that all energy is linked.

When I began to feel the effects of the healing products I was using on my cells, and that, because of this, my own behavior was changing, I realized this was not only profound, but also life changing.

The first modality I used on myself was Dr. Bach's remedies. These remedies are derived from natural plants. As such, they work in the body very easily, allowing us to shift our thinking naturally.

The second modality I used was hypnosis tapes, followed by transcendental meditation (TM) tapes. I have used a wide variety of hypnosis tapes. When working with my clients. I choose tapes that are appropriate to each situation. The tapes may vary—from past life regression to self-discovery to those designed to stop smoking or other undesirable habits. Transcendental tapes make use of sound and music designed to activate both sides of the brain, thus helping our brain to work more efficiently and more effectively.

Finally, I used essential oils made by Young Living. These oils contain the best, pure grade essential oils that I have found. I have also found that these oils work the best regarding the blood brain barrier.

Together, these four helpful tools (Bach Remedies, hypnosis tapes, TM tapes and essential oils) make up what I call the four modalities.

My personal interest in this project came about as I worked for eight years on my doctorate degree in clinical hypnosis. In the process, I worked with many clients who needed a longer-lasting result. Many asked if they could do follow-up work at home. Because I live in Alaska—and many people in Alaska suffer from seasonal affective disorder (SAD), which is caused by so much darkness—I observed the accumulation of personality problems from the long, dark winter. It seems that there is an accumulation of problems while living year after year in darkness that causes many more emotional problems than anywhere else in the United States.

This book is a compilation of my studies of the brain and how it can be affected by these modalities. The original intention of this book was for it to be a guideline for hypnotherapists to improve their practice by using incentive processes and products to facilitate a more life-changing result with their clients.

My hypnosis practice has mostly involved children, either those who are incest survivors or those with anger problems. I have also worked with couples, military personnel and sports athletes. I like to work with people for a short term, on a case-by-case basis. We usually utilize a thirteen-week window, wherein we cover—and use—all of the techniques covered in this book. Most often, thirteen weeks is enough time for the mind to free itself up easily. The problem resolves naturally. The client is then ready to go it alone.

The Basics

Energy

Electrical energy protects and helps the body survive the earth's magnetic pull. It helps us to feel healthier, such as when we spend time outdoors in a positive ion environment. We need extra stimuli to facilitate shifts in our lives. These stimuli help us to improve our thinking, invent new products, and bring us up to our higher potential.

For example, we become relaxed as we sit by the sea. This is due to a number of factors, including the ebb and flow of the tide. This ebb and flow is similar to the peristalsis of the body's flow. We are so connected to nature in so many ways that to commune with animals and feel what they feel is like communing with the gods. We are absolutely charged by all the energy around us.

Just watch how you feel when a negative person is around you. They are like a parasite, pulling all your own positive energy levels down. To be careful of these people may seem like a small task, but it is not. They are energy robbers, silently stealing all your positive thoughts and feelings. Sometimes, when they are done, you have to go to bed in order to survive the ordeal you have just been through. In the following pages, we will look at the energy forces that can help our bodies and minds to heal in a world that challenges us with so much negativity.

Using hypnosis as a Foundation

By combining hypnosis with other modalities, a practitioner's success can be phenomenal. We are the true mind/body experts of the new and transforming world. Hypnotherapists have already been using energy and have been aware of its powerful healing effects for years. It is already in our paradigm to help the client in as many arenas as we can. With essential oils, Bach remedies and meditation CD's, we can offer a complete energy treatment so that our client will achieve long-lasting results.

Using conscious hypnosis and other energy sources, we can facilitate a better result with our clients. As a group, hypnotherapists have been working with energy before it was so popular. All we need to do is add these other energy sources to our practice to further our results.

One example of nuts is by employing the modality of essential oils. If pure, these oils will pass through the blood-brain barrier and build up the immune system. They can help the body recover more quickly from the negative state. When used on a regular basis, a person will shift their life into a calmer state. The client who comes for help from the hypnotherapist needs a product that they can take with them. This will also make hypnotherapy sessions more powerful. With the oils, the client can go deeper in hypnosis. They can achieve a more effective life by using these oils daily.

Transforming Energy

As we transform the world with our technology, we must offer our clients as much as we can in modalities. Computer usage is at an all-time high. The electrical energy from these machines causes stress and drains the body. We have to offer our clients an alternative to this bombardment of negative energy. Untreated, our body does not rejuvenate every night. But, with essential oils and self-hypnosis, clients can go into a deeper REM state of sleep and be able to regenerate better. When they return to their computers, they are more productive and will feel better, which is the most important part of our clients' progress. They need to feel better on a consistent basis.

When trauma happens, an electrical charge is emitted into the body. The charge holds that trauma in the muscle, brain, body, mind and spirit experience until an unusual modality releases or moves the trauma. The consistency of the modality is very important. A regime of consistency throughout thirty to ninety days will unlock and lessen the trauma. In some cases, the trauma may even evaporate so that the person feels they have a new life.

Releasing Chakras

One modality will not do the trick for a lasting result. I encourage you to work with many chakras, meridians and essential oils. The chakras in our body are like two-way valves—they allow energy in and they allow energy out. However, if we are blocked by physical, emotional, mental or spiritual holds, our chakras will also hold these energies.

Because of this, it is important to clear the chakras every four hours so that we can be all we want to be in our lives.

Here is the schedule I use. In the morning, apply essential oils to the feet, heart, temples and in between the eyebrows. Four hours later, apply the oils to the heart, temples, outer perimeter of the ears and behind the ears. Four hours later, the oils can again be applied to the heart, temples and the top of the head. Before bedtime, apply the oils once again, this time to the feet, heart and perimeter of the ears.

As you work on applying oils to the chakras, a release happens. The more you use the oils specifically on these chakras, old holding memories or blocks get replaced with something better. Depending on the oils used, your organs will also begin to work better, more efficiently. By using the four-hour oil schedule, any negativity you may have picked up is released on a consistent basis. It is essential to understand that the body itself has memory. It can become a pleasure to release pent-up daily emotions with a fabulous essential oil.

Why We Need Consistency

When people go to motivational classes, the only way the program works is through follow-up CD's or a book so that the client can refresh his or her memory on the particular information. The brain has to be refreshed, and the process needs to be ongoing to change the behavior. It has to be consistent, every day. People lose momentum in the transition from the class to real life, so they need a boost. Their cells need the DNA and RNA to shift to a higher level so they can facilitate a change, but they need to be consistent. If part of the problem is genetic in nature this is especially important or the cell needs to remember only good energy.

Treating with the Four Modalities

In Search of a Better Life

There are approximately twelve million Americans on antidepressant medication in the world today. Numerous children are on Ritalin. Thousands of adults and children every year are put on various drugs to facilitate personality changes. These methods are not successful. People are incessantly searching for a better life.

One of the major reasons why I feel more work has such great validity is that so many of the children I have worked with have shifted their lives and the lives of their family. They have given up their anger for a better life. This methodology proves that with simple training, all clients can help themselves on a daily basis.

When working with the four modalities, clients are given simple instructions on each modality they are introduced to, one at a time. Every case is different and specific to each individual, as each individual is unique. Some clients require a 13-week window of consulting. This consists of personal coaching, helping the client to recognize where he or she wants to be as well as what results may be expected.

This method will attract many people because of the simplicity involved. In dealing with the four modalities, a number of questions may arise. Consultations may be necessary. At the same time, a client can easily become his or her own facilitator of this process by simply being consistent and using the Bach remedies or essential oils every four hours of the day. For this program to work, consistency is the key to long-term success.

Changes to Nature = Changes to Ourselves

Professor Gates, an instructor at Brigham Young University, said that essential oils and DNA have a great potential as natural products that may cure diseases. Natural product chemists and scientists are now willing to work more with the private sector. There are many more infectious diseases that can actually eat up DNA, thus causing our resistance to drugs that deal primarily with disease. One such strain is totally resistant to all antibodies, which is why essential oils are on the frontlines in combating infectious diseases. There are vast changes occurring because ecological forests are being destroyed. We are causing these diseases to happen because we are so interrelated with the earth. We need to pay more attention to how we treat our natural resources.

We also need to improve our quality of life. We need to care for our natural resources. The Amazon tropical resources include a vast parcel of land. We study these rainforests to learn the medicinal value of what is there. The world needs to see the dimension of what humans are going to need in the future. We are looking at essential oils to perfect our lives. In every plant, there is a special fungus. In the rain forest, we have no idea how these fungi work. In Tonga, there is a plant that may be anti-cancerous (affecting uterine cancer). Some plant compounds can affect hypertension. The National Institutes of Health need to recognize these compounds to better combat disease.

Essential Oils and DNA

The Art & Science of Essential Oils

Aromatherapy is an ancient art and science that is currently becoming more popular. It can create healing for many people that may not have had access to it before. With aromatherapy, attitudes can change and people can be supported through many crises. Degenerative disease can even be helped by essential oils. At times, oils can also be added to foods to help people return to health. What is important is getting the word out to people so they can help themselves.

There is a scientific pathway that leads to essential oils. In scientific studies, for example, an organism is grown in an aqueous solution. There is now a way to get essential oils to contact the organism and destroy it. Essential oil of oregano was tested in such a way against staph infection. Researchers found that the oregano oil killed staph in a petri dish. What was discovered was how the essential oil affects the organism. It was shown that oregano was more successful than regular antibiotics. Turkish oregano and melissa were tested with minimum inhibitory factors, and Turkish oregano was better when screened than regular antibiotics.

We know how important human life is, and essential oils will help us. Essential oils can improve our quality of life. We need to all work together to have this goal happen.

How Does It Work?

Oil is extracted from a plant and distilled through a long process to create an essential oil. Just as oils transport nutrients to plants, our blood works to transport nourishment and nutrients to our body. We need more oxygen in our blood and that's what essential oils add to our systems. Essential oils add oxygen and nutrients, and help to build up the immune system. Essential oils act as a transporter.

Essential oils go through the cell walls and deliver nutrients to the blood. The cell wall is receptive to essential oils, which in turn take in oxygen and nutrients. Essential oils have the ability to be the life force of the body because before they are oils they are the life force of a plant. Indeed, plants and their healing oils were the first medicine of man.

Our bodies vibrate with an electrical frequency. So do essential oils, having a vibration of 80 to 320 Hz. Most frequencies fracture the electrical energy around us. Essential oils have harmonic frequencies that help our bodies.

The electrical frequency in the body is lower a night than during the day. The foods and drinks we ingest affect our electrical frequency for the better or worse. Coffee, for example, lowers our frequency.

Disease starts at about 50 to 57 frequency. The ingestion through our skin of essential oils helps to regenerate and keep our frequency up. As a side effect, essential oils also stimulate our nerves—both to fire more effectively and to help repair damaged nerve endings.

Why We Need Essential Oils

Not only can we get oxygen from essential oils, we also get ions. Bacteria cannot live in ions. Our foods are saturated with chemicals; our aquifers are likewise contaminated. When ingested, these chemicals go into the intestinal tract. Thus, we unknowingly create a host for disease from these chemicals. Microbes can reproduce in twenty minutes. This causes a problem with antibiotic use. There is not one infection that can create a bacterium against an essential oil.

Because of the continual chemical poisoning of our food, water and environment, we have developed very weak immune systems. This, in turn, causes more illness. When and where will the next deadly virus occur? Local water supplies are not safe anymore. Many pathogens are lurking in our water supplies and our immune systems cannot fight them off. Essential oils help to re-establish cell activity and allow us to become healthier.

Preventing Disease

It has been known since ancient Egyptian times that essential oils are instrumental in fighting off disease. Moreover, essential oils can also help prevent disease. Lavender oil, for example, may fight against breast cancer. It can also be used as an effective treatment for allergies.

According to the French medical field, lemon oil has a chemical ingredient (sesquiterpenes) that goes beyond the blood-brain barrier. Because of this, essential oils may have the ability to help cure many serious diseases. Why? Because the oil increases oxygen as well as antibodies to help the body cure disease. In Europe, 150 hospitals use lemon oil for different reasons, including as a disinfectant and antibacterial agent. These oils contain the highest levels of oxygen.

Most Americans do not know that essential oils must be pure in order to work. In this respect, distillation is the most important aspect of creating an essential oil. Pure lavender oil is used widely in Europe for scalding burns, rheumatism and arthritis.

Are Essential Oils Safe?

Essential oils are totally safe, with no side effects. The olfactory system helps us breathe in the oil. From there, the oil molecule goes to the center of the brain, causing antibodies to form and protect the body. We get antifungal properties from inhaling oils. It is the most perfect air purification product available.

Some Examples of Essential Oils and Treatment

- Clary sage can help hormonal balance.
- In the Middle Ages, hyssop was used to protect children from the plague. (Some people feel the plague is not much different from AIDS. Yet we

have chosen to ignore this precious commodity's ability to help our body.)

- Helichrysum and birch are topical anesthetics. These oils also help loosen up negative emotions. In ancient times, a three-day ritual was used to eradicate evil spirits from the body. To help eradicate airborne bacteria, we can now use "purification," an oil blend.

- Cloves help stimulate the immune system.

- Frankincense is mentioned fifty-two times in the Bible. When taken into the body, essential oil of frankincense may help cure various forms of cancers and tumors. It is also helpful for people who become depressed.

- Rock rose oil helps eliminate viruses from the body. It is also a powerful agent in supporting the immune system.

Accumulative Effect

There are many formulas that support the immune system, which helps trauma to release from the DNA in cells. In turn, this may cause a profound life change that is consistent with a commitment to use the oils daily.

In all cases, the process is cumulative: the more we use the oils, the better we feel, the better our brain works and the more the immune system is supported and encouraged to help ward off disease.

DNA

Shifting Our Patterns

We now know that the body is affected by a blood transfusion and that our own blood cannot be identified by DNA testing for twenty-four to forty-eight hours until the other blood is integrated into our own. We also know that when a person is offered an organ for transplant (especially a heart), doctors inform the individual that he or she may wake up with a different personality because the organ came from another person. These examples show to what a great degree our DNA can be affected by what we put in our bodies.

In much the same way, essential oils, Bach remedies, hypnosis and TM CDs can shift our DNA—and our personality—for a short time. In the beginning, this may only last for a few hours to a day, but the more we shift and open to deeper levels, the more we shift our personality. There are subtle shifts that help our personality bring about even subtler behavioral changes. This seems to occur in stages: after thirty days of impact; after sixty days of impact; and after ninety days of impact. Once a lasting impact has been made on the personality, we will not return to the old behavior. This is life changing! For this reason, we cannot ignore the impact of the brain and the immune system.

Accepting Change

In the brain's "filing system," we have files from all stages of our life: from childhood through adolescence and adulthood. But these files can be redone (rewritten, as it were) by what we give our bodies for treatment.

Unlike its reaction to chemical medication, the bloodstream accepts natural treatments such as essential oils. In this way, the body more readily and easily accepts change. Why? Because the natural way is noninvasive: both the body and mind are, therefore, much more accepting of this process. On the other hand, medication is a foreign substance, a chemical that the body is forced to accept when our mind targets a particular situation. Many medications have time limits—you can only take them for so long and then you must stop. Also, in most cases, all medications do is suppress symptoms, not get rid of the cause. This paves the way to even more serious problems.

A Return to Nature

The natural way is most often better than the traditional Western medical way. In Tucson, Arizona, medical doctors can now take a course on alternative healing. Doctors learning about the art of natural healing—isn't this how it all started? More doctors are now interested in what all healers have known for centuries that when a substance is natural, the body is definitely more accepting of it. The body uses what it needs and then moves on to the next level of healing. The method is cumulative: the more you use the method, the better the results can be. In this way, trauma can be minimized, thus freeing up the mind and body to eradicate disease.

We are now taking notice of what temple priests, shamans and healers knew millennia ago that essential oils can and do work and are very easily accepted into the blood stream.

Physicians and psychiatrists now have to take a hard look at what they have been medicating their patients with. Many are not happy with the results. I think this is why we are beginning to see doctors shifting to study more natural healing modalities.

Becoming Responsible

Doctors often participate in their client's health much more than they really want to. Often, they are asked to make decisions for people that the patient should really be making for him or herself. Many people do not want to actively participate in their own health problems. They don't even want to ask questions. Or, if they do, they are often not the right questions. A person can be on five different medications and not even know the side effects of one, let alone what the combined side effects of five may be! Hormone therapy was popular for many years and now we find out it causes cancer.

The key is to make the client responsible. Sometimes it is important to ask who is responsible in each situation in order to decide what's next in a healing treatment. It is best for both client and healer to ask: What's next for the care of your body What's next for the care of your mind?

We have to take back our right to health care. We must be involved if we expect the best possible care for ourselves for we are the ones responsible for our own care. We must ask questions. We must be fully informed about side effects of medication. We must be willing to challenge what we have been given and ask why.

The Intuition Factor

Using Inner Knowing

We do not need to go through any stages for the brain, body and soul to respond to this process. We need only our inner knowing of what the client needs. We can read their energy level, their speaking and see how they carry their body to discover how to show them to use the modalities (and in what order) to help them. Hypnosis is the most important tool. How we see, feel and hear the client is our clue into what will take place. Likewise, the healer's voice in the process is probably the most important to the client. Are we compassionate? Are we understanding and nonjudgmental? The healing practitioner must filter out the garbage to find the core issue that will lead to successful treatment.

Usually a client who is very willing to proceed will have already had a variety of treatments that have failed. This type of client is willing to listen to anything to get a favorable result. For success to occur, the hypnotherapist must be willing to commit to the process and his or her client. Success comes from the energy exchanged between the two parties.

Creating a Positive Environment

When a parent has a child with Attention Deficit Disorder (ADD), for example, the energy exchanged is often so negative that the child does not have a chance to get better. I have sat with six ADD children without yelling or scolding them in any way. Eventually, they will sit with you and be calm and tell you about their lives. These children are so negatively charged, and so is their environment, that if they meet anybody who is conscious and positive, they are willing to be with this person. Children feel the energy fields of others. With an ADD child, you have only to open up the positive energy change and they will come forth.

The Body

The Value of Cleansing

We must cleanse our body daily to keep healthy. Fiber and enzymes are the most important in keeping plaque from building up in the system. Candida and parasites are big problems for our body.

Parasites

We are subject to parasites no matter what we eat. Do a cleanse to remove unwanted parasites so that your body's immune system has a chance to recuperate and rebuild. Essential oil of clove also may help rid the body of parasites. In addition, it will help the digestive system to become stronger. Rosemary oil is a great enzyme stimulator for better digestion. The more alkaline the body is, the more you burn fat. Low energy, bloating, fermentation, upper and lower gases, and skin eruptions are all signs of Candida, which is also a sign of parasites.

Candida

Yeast infections, recurring infections, hormonal imbalances and cancers are also all signs of a Candida problem. Eating foods that ferment in the digestive tract creates Candida. Taking minerals and drinking lots of water can greatly help treat Candida. However, it is important that the minerals can be absorbed correctly by the body. Enzymes must be produced to help the body digest correctly. When traveling, it is important to detoxify the body afterwards because of foods and parasites in different countries.

Creating Balance

We must maintain good intestinal flora. How do you know if your intestinal flora is good? If it isn't, your colon will not function correctly and will "bind up." We irritate our bodies by not allowing them to function correctly. We must have good flora so as not to have the body become toxic. One way to aid this is by improving colon hygiene. Colds and allergies are often a sign of a toxic colon. Eat with good digestive habits. One way is to eat fish. Do not eat dense protein after 3:00 P.M. unless you exercise a lot. After 3 P.M. it is difficult for the system to digest proteins properly and thoroughly; this leads to fermentation. The time period your body produces the most hormones is from 1:00 to 5:00 in the early morning.

Creating balance in the body is an important structure not only of the healing process but also in daily living. We must look at our bodies and evaluate the best program for ourselves. What we ingest affects the DNA of every cell. This, in turn, also affects our body.

We need to participate in the health of our body. Learn patience in creating a healthy body. It may take you ten to fifteen years to become completely healthy. If you want to have health and rebuild your life, you must participate in your health. We have to be awake to what's needed and participate fully in our body, mind and spirit connection.

The Amazing Cell

Can Cells Think?

The cell divides by mitosis, but what tells the cells to divide? Can a cell think for itself? If so, what are the consequences? Just as our thoughts affect our health, physically and psychologically, can a cell's thoughts affect our entire being?

I believe that each cell actually has a mind of its own. That is why the triggers I teach people to use work so quickly. They help the cell to not only be healthier but think healthier. This is a cutting-edge process that can actually revolutionize hypnotherapy.

Humans have learned how to clone animals from cells. When we clone, are we telling that cell to do something that, at the cellular level, the cell already knows how to do? The cell must think for itself if it has the power to clone itself given the right conditions. We are on the threshold of technology in coming to understand and appreciate the amazing cell.

Miracles

We have all been mind and body experts for years but we did not know it! Hypnosis generates many health benefits. Miraculous healing happens as people pray about their cancer or illness. An accident happens and people miraculously heal themselves.

A client of mine weighing 110 pounds was crunched by a snow machine. Her clavicle was dislocated. The doctors gave her no hope of healing. Through exercise, diet and sheer willpower, she is now fine.

These healings are so profound that science sometimes has to take a back seat. Cloning is the new proof that cells do indeed have miraculous qualities. The cell is encouraged to produce something and it does exactly that.

Deep Thoughts

When a client undergoes hypnosis, the heart rate slows down and the mind goes into an altered state of consciousness. The client can begin to unveil problems that could not easily be handled under normal consciousness.

Because the subconscious never sleeps, the mind is constantly processing information. The body is the recipient of these messages. So, the body is responding all the time to the mind's stimulus. When clients are put on psychotropic drugs, they give the body the message to withhold emotion. This can cause disease to happen in the body because this is not a natural response. The message at the cellular level is that we are not allowed to process. If not allowed to respond naturally, we will most often respond negatively.

Restoring Personality at the Cellular Level

Most drugs given to help depression are only suppressing the problem, so when the client is taken off the drug the same problem remains. Many times the problem is now even larger since the client was unnaturally forced to suppress it in the first place. The same problem is now magnified, multiplied by years of suppression. This means that the original personality has been altered. The healing practitioner must work on trying to restore the personality to its original state. To do this, natural modalities must be employed. These include Bach remedies, essential oils, hypnosis and transcendental meditation (TM). These modalities are gentle and soothing to a confused psyche. It will take a committed facilitator, someone who is willing to listen to all the garbage that has been collected to get to the root of the problem.

This work is very fulfilling and has great rewards. The body has somatic response to trauma; it holds the trauma until it can be released. Some modalities allow the body to release the trauma. The more consistent the modality, the more the trauma is released, allowing the body to function better.

The modality is actually speaking to the cell at the cellular level. No matter what the DNA is, there is a shift in the mind as the modality takes over the body. Our mind can facilitate any change if we allow ourselves the change. Our mind is so complex but our subconscious never sleeps. Whatever we feed it, it picks up on and the mind will shift completely if we are consistent in applying the modality for a period of thirty to ninety days. Our behavior can change if we allow it to, but sometimes we are the products of our environment and we stay the same out of what we know. We do not have to stay there, however. We have a choice.

Clarity

Becoming Clear

There is a cleansing that takes place when a facilitator is very sure of his or her work. In other words, when there is clarity, cleansing may occur.

I once took a kinesiology class called Truell technology. During the class, another student was having obvious trouble. After the class, I went home and treated three clients and noticed that I could clear myself very quickly between clients. The next day, I shared my technique with my classmate. He tried the technique and found that it worked just as easily and quickly for him as it did for me.

Here is the technique that I use: First, allow yourself to relax. It is important not to have any thoughts in your mind. Begin with a simple hands-on touching of each chakra. Then, place your left hand on your forehead and rub gently while lightly tapping your chest with your other hand. Allow yourself to release any tensions, any troubles. When you feel the release, take three deep breaths.

Approximately ten minutes of this technique will clear anyone of anything. It also works very well to encourage mental alertness.

Special Sensing Abilities

Some people possess the ability to see or feel things differently than others. These individuals can often feel or see trauma; they are very tuned in. Often, these people can tell, just by a look, whether there is sadness or pain or blockage in another person. They may be able to sense the type of help that is needed. These individuals often have higher body heat and energy levels than others. They have the ability to help others at a level that may not be available to other facilitators who have not been trained to do so. This is definitely a gift, but all people possess this innate ability. However, people need to be trained in this ability.

In training to open to this ability, we learn to still the mind and be in a place where there are no judgments, nor any preconceived thoughts. This stillness brings forth more success in treating clients since the practitioner is not judging. They can sense if the practitioner harbors judgment or. Clients know this limited thoughts. In effect, the practitioner is an open channel to the success of the treatment.

In working with clients, our energy field needs to be clear at all times so that our work can be powerful. This ability also leaves us open to new information that earlier may not have been available. When a practitioner opens on this level, he or she will just be listening and the client will volunteer the needed information. We may even think to ourselves: *Did I need to know that? Isn't it a coincidence that I found out just what I needed to know?* As we maintain this level of clarity at all times, this natural unfolding of information will happen much more often and much more easily.

Maintaining Clarity

As healing practitioners, we must not be swayed by people who try to steal our energy through their own negative thoughts, actions and words. It is important to always clear one's self after each session and constantly build energy back up to a clear, refreshing level. Because this work attracts people who need help in healing, it also attracts people who will, if given the chance, deplete the practitioner's energy. We must all revitalize ourselves daily.

Ways to Revitalize

- Meditate daily for thirty to forty-five minutes.
- Use essential oils of your choice to ward off negativity every four hours.
- Use Bach remedies; walnut is especially effective in warding off negative people.
- Drink lots of water.
- Use karma hypnosis CDs or past life CDs, whichever one helps the most (I personalize these CDs for my clients, though you can also create your own personalized CDs.)
- When living in a city, plan trips to the countryside; sit and interact with nature to regain your center.
- When in a communication where negativity shows up, do not allow yourself to have an opinion. This

will deflect the energy and give the other person ownership of their negativity.

- When meeting with people with too much external energy, back away, listen and do not take on their problems. These people are racing through life in a circle of confusion that leads nowhere. Usually these people are very materialistic and find no value in their fellow man.

Personality

Personality is an ever-changing ordeal. We are always looking for the right answers. Do we ever find them? This is our quest. The question we must answer is can we free up our personality to be different?

The Power of Suggestion

Children adapt easily to our suggestions because they have no ready agenda about us to stop them. Children (when accompanied by parents) can easily be hypnotized with successful results. One seven-year-old girl came to see me with her mother for incest problems. Within a twenty-minute suggestion period, the child entered an altered state of consciousness, as did her mother. After a guided exercise, the child awoke to share very explicit details, sharing a trust in both her mother and my- self that transcended her trust in others. She was fine for many months afterward, having only two treatments.

We know that the power of suggestion is great, but children surpass the limits of language early on. They can, through conscious hypnosis, feel, sense and intuit your actual intent. Children want to be helped.

We can facilitate so much in humans. We just need to realize the energy fields that we are dealing with. We need to learn to recognize at what level the person's energy functions and where they want changes. We must also ask ourselves: Are they wiling to change? Is there a trust level that will facilitate a change within them?

The Wall of Resistance

Do not be fooled by a child's resistance. After all their protests, they will eventually listen deep in their heart of hearts. Most children desperately want help. Sometimes they are crying out for help; we only need to listen. In my experience, children aged seven to twelve are the best subjects, though even thirteen is a very willing age.

One thirteen-year-old girl I worked with was very angry. She was smoking marijuana and beating up other girls at school. She came to see me with her grandmother. It took four sessions and some regression work, but finally she broke down. In the following thirteen weeks, she became a much better student and was more cooperative at home. To date, she attends a Christian school, plays the piano and receives straight A's.

I never allowed this girl's poor attitude to stand in the way of what I knew my work could bring about. I always live in the space of conviction that the treatment will work. Because of this, I knew that there would eventually be a breakthrough. When it happened, this girl's face began to look very different as she became in touch with the love that she is. She could share herself in spiritual ways that she was previously unable to do.

If we began to view these children as God's gift to us, how many children's lives could we help to change?

I feel it is important to note here once again how very crucial it is to include the child's parents or grandparents in treatment. Always, this work is best when it includes the full environmental circle that surrounds the child's everyday life.

Listening with Attention

With children, the beginning trauma is what causes the problem. We must listen for the core trauma. We do not ask for it. Rather, the child shares it out of the work we do. It is shared in the trust we create in the parameters of the work. One of the greatest things is to gain the trust of the child. Once done, they endear themselves to us. Our work is ever so important. We are thrusting out into new terrain: the energy path. We can help repair a child's energy field, giving that child the sense that a new life can be found. They will feel hope is available if we dare to push forward and help them.

Work with Children

A basic plan

Children are very easy to work with, for they have no hidden agendas. It is only trauma that stops children in life. Work with their goals and they will blossom easily. They are not stopped by old behavior. Almost every angry child has an old unresolved trauma. Treat the trauma and the anger goes away. The real child is then revealed. When working with children, parents and/or grandparents must also be treated at the same level as the child.

When working with children, I use the following program:

- Trauma: I first work to identify the trauma within the child. Together, we work to release this trauma easily. Depending on the situation, we may use essential oils or the Bach remedies. "Trauma Life" is often a very helpful essential oil when working with trauma. Dr. Bach's "Rescue Remedy" is also effective, especially in helping the child to relax and share his or her true feelings.

- Anger: With angry children, I always start with an essential oil called "Acceptance" and a night-time oil called "Dream Catcher" so that REM sleep may be restful. If the child can feel different he or she will begin to act differently. Oftentimes, a child will ask for the essential oil or remedy because it works so well.

- Modality: You will learn to discover which combination of essential oils and Bach remedies works best for each individual. Many choices are obvious. For an individual who is easily distracted, for example, use oils and remedies that enhance brain focus, encourage rest and relaxation, and level out emotional mood swings.

- Conscious Hypnosis: For this aspect of the program, I follow the approach that the language we use to speak is what we become. Thus, what we say to others is what they may become. Use your words consciously as you interact with your clients.

- Remedies: A certified Bach practitioner may recommend Bach remedies. Another approach is to study these remedies yourself. By using the remedies, you will soon learn which are appropriate in each situation. The remedies are all safe and especially effective on children. In general, Bach remedies help children to relax and work through their life issues more easily and effectively.

- Transcendental Meditation CDs: These tapes are helpful in that the effects stay with each individual for thirty-six hours or more. Overactive children may especially benefit and gain additional focus while using these tapes.

- Success: How successful you are depends upon your consistency. When working with children, you must reinforce this consistency every four hours. In addition, when you interact with the child, it is important to speak and act as though you are having success. Most importantly, never give up! We all need someone to believe in us every minute of every day, especially children.

- Graphology and Handwriting Exercises: I also work with the child's handwriting, doing positive statements about who they really are.

This program is very effective, and the practitioner will get results fast. When working with clients, I don't discuss the trauma. A basic knowledge of the trauma is all that is needed. I use intuition to discover what the client needs. Most often, the client will reveal the most pressing needs through sharing. Also, I proceed slowly. It is important to gain the client's trust before healing can begin to occur.

Parents can develop their own version of this process easily. They just have to want the knowledge and be willing to use and model consistency. It is important for practitioners to see the child and parent at the same time, for this will be the level at which they will shift.

The parent must have no known agenda. This process will work, but the parent and practitioner must allow it to work. As hypnosis professionals, we already have the mind/body connection paradigm as a framework that we work with all the time. We all have the energy and intuitiveness to work successfully with clients.

Identifying Trauma

We must first listen to what the trauma really is. When working with children, the practitioner must see the trauma point in the child from the past to the present. Most often this will invariably include the parents.

A child and his or her parents each have a dynamic that must be treated simultaneously. If only the child is treated, the success rate will be very low. If only the adult is treated, the success rate will be a little higher, but not the best it can be, and certainly not what we are looking for.

A parent most often has expectations of what type of outcome can result from a trauma. A child, however, has not worked this through and does not know how to communicate the problem or trauma to his or her parents. Therefore, a negative dynamic forms and continues on for some time—maybe years. The child becomes resentful and uncooperative. He or she may lose interest in school, friends, and family—maybe everything. The child most often has a lot of anger.

When I see these children, I do not listen to the parent. I only listen to the child in order to find the root of the problem. One way I facilitate a breakthrough is to have the parent present in the session, though not sitting with the child. At these sessions, we do goal setting and the child talks about his or her goals. Together, we look to the future for the child. Many of these children have terrific goals, but no one is listening.

Specifics

To get the child to cooperate, I use Dr. Bach's remedies. A good place to start is with Rescue Remedy. This must be used on a daily basis. I also recommend an essential oil called Motivation. When rubbed into the skin, this oil passes through the blood/brain barrier and helps the child to feel better and think more clearly.

I also recommend that a TM CD be used. These tapes will help the right and left sides of the brain to work more harmoniously together so that the child can feel fully present. This child now knows the future does exist and the trauma need no longer stop progress. In the parameters of this process with some of the children, I use regression CDs, but this depends on the age of the child and the energy I intuit in the situation. By using intuition, most hypnotherapists will know when to utilize regression CDs.

The parent must also be treated with an oil modality or remedy so as to reach the same healing level the child is on. The parent may also need extensive coaching in his or her negative behavior. However, during sessions we never label this behavior. Parents need to feel this therapy will work. They need to have hope that their child will have a better life. This is extremely important, and the parent must participate in their child's treatment. If they do not, treatment will not succeed.

For this reason, negative language on the part of the parent must be stopped. If you notice a parent saying something like, "My child has ADD," kindly ask that the parent discontinue this labeling. Educate the parent to replace certain limiting terminology with more positive comments. By example, the child can learn this as well.

Lastly, it cannot be stated enough times that the parent and the child must be consistent every day in this process for it to work.

Case Histories

When treating a child, parents need first to look for the root of the problem. Stress triggers so much in children, in everything from asthma to stomach disorders. Parents can easily help their children with their modalities if they have a commitment to consistency.

One mother I worked with presented with the problem of one of her four-year-old twins. The child had awakened in the middle of the night and was unable to breathe from an asthma attack. I asked if the child had any stress. At first, the mother said no, but upon further conversation it was revealed that another child had been hitting her at day care. The child, coming from a loving home, did not know what to do about it. The child who had been hitting came from a dysfunctional family embroiled in a divorce situation. The mother was encouraging her daughter to hit back, which is really not an appropriate response. I recommended that the mother begin rubbing her daughter's feet with "Raven," a formula that helps to open up the respiratory system. Also recommended was the use of a misting vaporizer at night in the child's bedroom to help her relax.

Over time, the mother began to see spectacular results. She realized that stress could indeed induce a great many reactions in children. I told this woman, "Your children came from a good environment, so don't look at the symptom—look to the root. Look for the stress that induced the problem and you will have great results when you deal with it."

A Client's Letter of Thanks

Here is letter from a mom who has discovered the beneficial ways in which essential oils have helped her child:

Dear Kathy,

I would like to extend to you my sincere thanks for introducing me to essential oils. Here's a little story.

My six-year old daughter is very active, both day and night. Keeping up with her has been exhausting. Last fall, she became very interested in her doctor kit and "playing check-up." She frequently commented that her "heart is beeping." By January, she was still playing with her medical bag. She developed a cold that lingered on into a sinus infection. One of her visits to the doctor showed cause for her medical bag. She was feeling her heart rate, which was noted to be 130 to 150 beats per minute.

For nearly a year, we have been looking for ways to calm her down to where she can rest and stay focused on the task or activity at hand. She's been up and down several times a night more often than I care to admit. Her dad has said, "She's 220 in a 110 world."

Update: I've been using the oils on my daughter for about two weeks now. About 20 minutes after rubbing oil on her feet at night, she's drifting off to sleep. On occasion, she'll wake up once during the night (most often, it is 7:30 in the morning!)

I've also been using oils throughout the day to help achieve a sense of calm. By the second day, when we sat down to watch a video, she sat down and watched an en- tire feature length movie. That's a first!

What is really awesome is that when my daughter feels "cranky" or "not happy," she comes to me and by the time I get my oils she's there waiting with her wrists extended.

I've also noticed changes in myself. I'm a migraine suffer and have difficulty falling asleep. By using oils on my daughter, I've also reaped many benefits and I am able to rest and fall asleep without using a sleep aid. What a blessing!

My son and husband have felt the benefits of the oils and aromas in our home as well. I personally have felt my stress level drop drastically since I've started using them on my daughter.

Thank you again,

Teresa Liberty
Valdez, Alaska

Hi Ms. Kathy,

I just wanted to take a moment to share how amazing you've been for my daughters in Kindergarten, First and Second grade.

Since they started working with you, I've seen such a big difference in their grades and overall progress in school. But what really stands out is how much more confident they've become. They're more willing to try, speak up, and take on new challenges without getting discouraged.

You've also done a great job helping them build their vocabulary and really understand what they're learning, not just memorize it. It's clear you take the time to make sure things click for each of them in a way that works.

What I really appreciate is that you push them to strive for excellence while still being supportive and encouraging. That balance is exactly what they needed, and it's made a huge impact on their growth.

Most importantly, you've created a really positive environment for them, and they genuinely enjoy their sessions with you—which says a lot!

I'm so grateful for everything you've done and couldn't recommend you more.

Thanks so much,
A'Jha Thomas

Conclusion

What to Expect

In doing this work and following their program with consistency, adults and children will change behavior. Why? Because we are working at the cellular level. In this particular time in our history, we are on the cutting edge of how we can affect DNA. We can actually help our cells change at the cellular level. Essential oils, for example, can penetrate the blood/brain barrier. However, we must be consistent. Any process must be used every day, every four hours, for at least thirty to ninety days in order to effect a shift in the brain and cells. Our cells have memories ingrained in them. The brain also has cells and memories that cannot be shifted merely by someone telling you to shift them.

It is consistency that is the key in helping us to shift at a cellular level and, thus, have remarkable success. When working with children, it is particularly important that the parents follow the same process as the child. If the parent fails to do so, the child will not have success. The dynamics created by the parent and child have to be changed in order for either one to shift. A shift will happen when the parent is consistent with themselves and with their child.

I have found in working with clients that it is essential we all work together. Once this happens, clients become naturally more balanced and centered in life.

Things became easier for them. Consequently, the client's whole well being is affected.

Summary

In summary, when we work with the bloodstream and the brain, we facilitate a lasting shift that helps all of our organs to work better. The brain has a better thought pattern. The cells have a more pleasant memory, and the muscles release all of our negative trauma. We begin to feel better and look better. All of our old trauma gets released from our body, down to our very cells.

What could be better than to practice this system?

After all, what have your little cells got to lose?

Points to Remember

- Bach remedies, transcendental meditation CDs and other modalities by themselves will help to shift a client, but it's the whole pie that really works best, not just one single slice.

- The facilitator must be very clear in this work because the client can feel your thoughts. If you do not have a commitment to a particular person, do not work with him or her. The healing process will not work if that individual doubts your seriousness and commitment.

- Do not allow yourself to become affected by the chaos the person may be presenting. See it as that individual's experience. Have no judgments on this and your client will have miraculous recoveries out of your nonjudgmental attitude.

- Stay with our client, especially children. Take the time to let children shift with their parents because they will! Children really intuit commitment at a very deep level; when you love and trust them, they will shift.

- Stay clear when working with this process and the results will flow in!

Remember

- You can affect the energy emitting from a DNA pattern.

- DNA energy is a life force that can be shifted.

- As the energy emitting from the DNA patterns shifts, the behavior of an individual shifts.

To believe is to conceive a new level of conscousness!

- We are embarking on a new frontier.

- This is only the beginning for all of us.

- Our DNA patterning is not holding us; rather, it is the pathway to our genius.

- Each of us has a genie in the bottle waiting to come out.

- We have only to be our own physician and to heal our body~mind~spirit to experience a quantum leap in our lives.

If I can do it, anyone can do it!

You need only to get started!

Danielle Strough
Assistant Principal
Signature Preparatory
dstrough@signatureprep.org

May 5, 2025

To Whom It May Concern,

It is with great pleasure that I write this letter of recommendation for Kathy Reddick. Kathy has been an integral part of our team at Signature Preparatory, initially joining us as a substitute teacher. From day one, she seamlessly filled in wherever needed, demonstrating a natural ability to adapt, connect with students, and support learning in any classroom setting.

Two years ago, we were fortunate to transition Kathy into a full-time paraprofessional role, working with some of our most behaviorally intensive special needs students. This work is challenging and requires immense patience, empathy, and resilience—qualities that Kathy embodies every single day.

Kathy consistently works with students who demonstrate high levels of need, including those who elope from the classroom, exhibit physical aggression, or show significant defiance. She approaches each situation calmly and professionally, creating safe, structured environments where students feel supported. One of her greatest strengths is her ability to think outside the box—Kathy tailors her approach to each student, honing in on what they specifically need to succeed. Whether it's using sensory tools, movement breaks, visual schedules, or quiet connection time, Kathy adjusts her strategies to help each student stay focused, regulated, and engaged.

Her ability to build trust and form meaningful one-on-one relationships with students has had a transformative impact on their progress and behavior. Kathy is dependable and creative—qualities that make her a true asset to any school team.

I wholeheartedly recommend Kathy Reddick for any role supporting students, particularly those who require intensive behavioral and academic support. She brings heart, dedication, and an individualized approach to everything she does.

Sincerely,
Danielle Strough

Assistant Principal
Signature Preparatory